love in reverse, to play in traffic as all the cars swerve around our magic, to question the role of any one life. *Hero Victim Villain* is a scrounging-about in parts of the mind which let loose our hearts upon the lovely little holy and immaculate moments.
 — Jessica Rigney, Author of *Within Poetic Boxes*

Ably abetted by plain language, like letters from a friend, and allowing for oddities like playing in traffic and getting chased by skeletons, Maiurro orchestrates poetic hiraeth like few others. The effect is intoxicating, and will knock you for a loop, "and elsewhere as you finish the last line of your best poem you realize, this is not the holy moment. They all are."
 — Alexandra Naughton, Author of
 American Mary

In this book, damn him, Brice knows secrets we all keep tucked away, and shares them without asking permission. Lucky for us he is mostly benevolent. He draws a charcoal map of his mind and leads us to rest on the knife edge where love meets fear. Brice grabs us readers gently but urgently by the hand, pausing to shine light wherever the humdrum meets the infinite.
 — Sarah Larue, Author of
 i'll just hide until it's perfect

"I defenestrated a television set which only played one o'clock infomercials and I made a bed for poems in its place." Indeed. I so want to quote every line of this wildly clever, deeply auspicious book which I began reading 'round 1am and could not stop 'til every page had been turned. How does a writer pull so many spot-on prophetic, wisely emotional, oft funny poems out of one head? While magically traversing so much turf of life? By being Brice Maiurro, of course. His *Hero Victim Villain* has found its place on the fave top shelf of books I will continue to read, well into the night.
 — Roseanna Frechette, Poet

This vital, dynamic collection begs to be read aloud. Maiurro's use of rhythm paired with keen internal observation makes this book a must-read.
  — Jenn Zuko, Professor of Writing,
    Denver University, Professional Ninja

Maiurro, with burned fingers and singed eyebrows, extinguishes the very fire he sparked to life. Our "prophet of emotion", Maiurro presents raw and sludgy time-lapse footage of what has become of us. Both rewind and skip "soaking in the mushy grossness of love." How different will you perceive the sweater engulfed by ash only to have it gripping your back again, unfrayed? This is okay. This is fine.
  — C.C. Hannett, Author of *Triune*

Brice Maiurro is a river. Uncontrollable, raging, and replenishing. You can't take a sip out of Brice because he'll leave you thirsting for more. He once wrote a poem about talking to God in a coffee shop and teaching God a lesson. He is soft, rippling, and cutting. He can love the hardness right out of someone and he has. Brice is what rushing water dreams to sound like when it grows up.
  — Varinia A. Rodriguez, Author of
    The Jellyfish Dream

In response to the victim/villain/hero triangle, it is said that you break the triangle by saying how you feel and what you want. I believe that Brice does just that throughout these pages. At times, I find myself laughing at the irony and at other times rekindling my own sense of longing, which for me, only happens when experiencing poetry that is both clear and vulnerable. He illustrates every day imagery with complex emotion which makes his poetry not only accessible, but also so very memorable.
  — Whitney Beth Harris, Poet

More Praise for *Hero, Victim, Villain*

Our poetry is short on truth-telling these days, but high on aesthetics. Finally, we have Brice Maiurro. This collection is no-bullshit, accessible, and like a companion who has heard your agonies and reflects them back to the world. In conversation with poets like Eileen Myles and CA Conrad, the stanzas here are a persistent reframing of what we think we know about ourselves and the places we end up. When I read, "Boulder is getting a Tarot reading from Charles Schwab," I know we have a poet who isn't afraid of humor, or of shining a light on our own absurdities, which is greatly needed. Being without this collection is like being without a torch in a very dark wood.
— Blake Edward, Author of *12x12 and Other Stories*

This striking second collection of poetry from Brice Maiurro is full of hope, humor, and heartache. *Hero Victim Villain* chronicles a poet finding his voice and footing in an oftentimes chaotic and overwhelming world -- ultimately embracing life, one self-inflicted punch to the face at a time.
— Steve Shultz, Author of *FM Ghost*

Brice Maiurro has quickly become one of the most pervasive names in the Denver literature scene. His caustic wit, emotional urgency, and lyrical wizardry are just as intoxicating at a live reading as on the printed page. Those who love the dizzying imagery of Howl or the celestial hedonism of William Blake will feel right at home with *Hero Victim Villain*.
— Josiah Hesse, Author of *The Carnality Series*

Sibylline and resounding, *Hero Victim Villain* asks that its reader crash-land without a helmet. Maiurro's poems gut tenderly, leaving you lustful and indebted to identity and the world that feeds it.
— Ahja Fox, Poet

Maiurro's *Hero Victim Villain* is an exercise in stream of consciousness that somehow draws all the parts of the reader--you: the hero, you: the victim, you: the villain--in all at once, in every

poem. The poet's knack for pulling internal reflection outside of itself and making the poet's personal both relatable and tangible to the reader is an experience best consumed aloud--you may find it difficult to distinguish your own voice from Maiurro's as you nod in agreement the whole way through.
— Erica Hoffmeister, Author of *Roots Go Wild*

Brice Maiurro's voice is so familiar, it might be yours. You've never met, yet you recognize him immediately. You've been waiting your whole life for permission like this. To be a person. Any person. A better one. It's not that his writing is magic, it's that you are, and he knows it. This book does not want anything from you but to be alive and happy. You are beautiful, whatever you think that means. Brice is your co-conspirator, your secret self. Forever after, when you look in the mirror, poetry is what you'll find.
— Eric Fischman, Author of
Mordy Gets Enlightened

Brice Maiurro claims with a soft force, "this is not the holy moment/they all are" and in this one small line in the middle of many long, urgent, poems that are at times conversations with himself and this world and waiters and friends at tables and burning images, I agree. His poems are at the same time funny and existential, but not in the way you think. Every time Maiurro makes a pithy, wildly mundane but also fantastical statement full of images that take me into several dimensions of thought and reverie, I smile because even when it's dark, I feel holy in his poems. Brice Maiurro reminds me it's all holy, every time.
— Tara Shea Burke, Poet and Teacher

All the apertures of a mind we may access, yet we do not. Fortunate for us, Brice Maiurro luxuriates among the perforations of thought. His rhythmic narrations of self-interrogation heave thoughts upon our laps one after another until without notice, beauty offers us a bus stop gentleman proclaiming "Ring ring! Ring ring!" Brice gives us the opportunity to answer, to fall in

HERO
VICTIM
VILLAIN

Hero Victim Villain

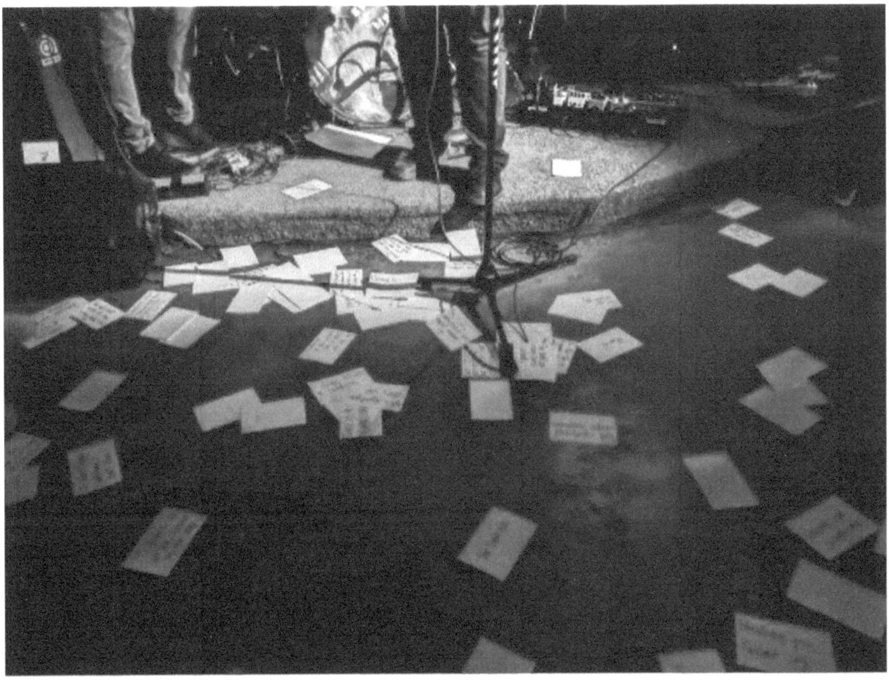

poems by

Brice Maiurro

STUBBORN
MULE
PRESS
DEVIL'S ELBOW, MO

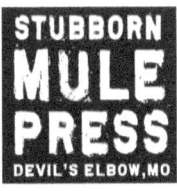

Stubborn Mule Press
Devil's Elbow, MO
stubbornmulepress.com

All poems copyright © Brice Maiurro, 2019

First Edition 11 7 5 3 2 1
ISBN: 978-1-950380-31-2
LCCN: 2019942218
Design, edits and layout: Jeanette Powers
stubbornmulepress@gmail.com @stubbornmulepress
CoverArt: Elim J Sidus
Interior Photo: Julia Bryan
Bio Photo: Matt Diss, ALOC Media

Are you really reading this? Congratulations, we love you. No one but the author can really claim rights to their work, no matter what law says what. And we can't really do anything about theft, whatever that means, so here is our pact: Be cool, be kind, don't steal, email the author if you like or want to riff off their work. Also, let us at Stubborn Mule know if you want to write a review, we'll share it and your review publication, too. Go ahead and use passages for reviews, accolades, or epigraphs, give credit where credit is due. Let's stay radical, share with us our honor among anarchists.

To a white bird.

Thank you to Whitney Beth Harris, who shared with me that she once was told we all play the hero, the victim and the villain sometimes, and sometimes that's okay.

Poem Publications

The Canary Who Swallowed The Coal Mine – *Horror Sleaze Trash*
Enter The Cartoon Bluebirds – *Stain'd Arts*
Defenestration – *Stain'd Arts*
Boulder – *Suspect Press*
Why I Write Poetry – *Horror Sleaze Trash*
Variations on a Complaint in a Restaurant – *Stain'd Arts*
The Tilt – *Spit Poet*
Death Disease – *Stain'd Arts*
The Eight of Swords – *Anti-Heroin Chic*
How To Be Alive – *Stain'd Arts*
Shave Your Beard and Go Home, Sam – *Anti-Heroin Chic*
The Eight of Swords – *Anti-Heroin Chic*

Table of Contents

The Canary Who Swallowed the Coal Mine - - - - - - - 13
Enter the Cartoon Bluebirds - - - - - - - - - - - - - 17
Defenestration - - - - - - - - - - - - - - - - - - - 18
Boulder - 22
Why I Write Poetry - - - - - - - - - - - - - - - - - 25
How to Punch Yourself in the Face - - - - - - - - - - 27
Variations on a Complaint in a Restaurant - - - - - - - -32
The Inbetween - 35
A Self-Analysis - - - - - - - - - - - - - - - - - - - 38
The Tilt in the Axis of the Earth - - - - - - - - - - - 41
Broken-Winged Bird - - - - - - - - - - - - - - - - - 42
That One Week Where I Thought I Had The Death Disease -44
The Apple Store - - - - - - - - - - - - - - - - - - -47
Bus Stop Koan - 49
Dear Human, -50
Hero -51
Sound Reverberated Off of Mountains - - - - - - - - - 53
Bar Rhapsody -56
Clone - 61
Bukowski, again - - - - - - - - - - - - - - - - - - - 62
Snippet of a Man Talking About His New Television Set - - 64
The Eight of Swords - - - - - - - - - - - - - - - - - 65
We Could Fall in Love in Reverse - - - - - - - - - - -66
And in The Red Corner of This Here Life - - - - - - - 70
Heaven - 72
How To Be Alive - - - - - - - - - - - - - - - - - - - 73
Shave Your Beard And Go Home, Sam - - - - - - - - 76
Dear Audience, - - - - - - - - - - - - - - - - - - - 77
Unlistened-To Voicemails - - - - - - - - - - - - - - -78
Love Poem for Everything - - - - - - - - - - - - - - 80

The Canary Who Swallowed the Coal Mine

Everything is on fire and I want to sleep for at least two weeks
so drown me in Zzzquil and read to me
from your Gideon's Bible.

Read me something simple that tastes like reality.
Read me a story that is less Christian and more inarguably true

because everything is on fire and I want to
sleep for at least two weeks maybe more but
I understand the shit green cloud of fiscal
responsibility is hanging over my head like
a drunk woman pouring buckets of water out
of her tenth story Brooklyn window.

When I say everything is on fire, I mean *everything is on fire*.

The couch cushions are on fire, the fruit stands are on fire
and it never rains anymore.

All seven of the televisions inside of my skull are on fire.
The intravenous highways of the United States are on fire.
They IV drip down entitlement and God complexes
hero complexes.

My hero complex is on fire, my victim mentality is on fire,
my love for strangers.

The cat is on fire and it's still too afraid of the water to go in it.

(I am the cat in this scenario
and the water is a therapist
or any variety of activities that
require coming to your senses)

but why would I go see a therapist

when I know the therapist is on fire?

Their fainting couch on fire
their perfectly framed doctorate on fire

and this is why I want to sleep.

The cross was set on fire by the pastors
the oil slick ocean is still burning

The devil is on fire, he's so fucking confused
he's just pacing and pacing in my head in your head
in most everyone's heads which too are on fire.

I find it hard to sleep to the sound of the eleven o'clock news.

I find it close to impossible
to rationalize an escape plan in a fun house.

I find myself easily a victim to sensory overload and I realize
that it's maybe inescapable

we've built flashing lights into every dark alley
always on camera, the flag is on fire, media on fire
death is on fire, religion on fire
the Buddhists are on Facebook again
the streets are like a giant block party

a giant pool party,

except with fire

and in the ocean of it all,
I feel something with you
and I worry that too is fleeting
or possibly completely imaginary
you tell me you're allergic to dogs while I pant incessantly
while I shit on your carpet and you hit me with a rolled-up

newspaper
but you let me lay beside you on the couch
and I dream
like that age we all once were where we were so good at it
where it was nothing much less than unlearned behavior
but now

the paintings are on fire.

I think about my childhood friend
a Jackson Pollack painting, on fire
I think about her alcoholic paint drizzle
the way she'd spontaneously combust
like a Kerouac star,
(none of this is aggrandizement).

I remember the way she'd piece back together
I think about how part of why I left her
is she wore that t-shirt on the outside
that I kept swallowed.

I'm good at swallowing things
even when they're on fire.

I swallow jazz records
I swallow momentary relapses of judgement, insanity pleas.

I swallow the attention of strangers
who don't love me they love the poet
they love me in two dimensions, on fire
in slick acrylic bursts of orange red and yellow

and I love them the same way sometimes but I worry
and sit by a fireplace while inside of a fireplace
and that fireplace is a brick city where tourists live
and somehow overnight I became the unfamiliar one
in the city that I love.

The newer transplants tell me the good spots to grab a coffee
where the WiFi is tasty and well-seasoned
they tell me how terrible the drivers are
they can't see that I'm on fire
and that's okay because I can't see them
I can't see anything but this delicate eggshell heart
floating up to the sky

as I drift into two week sleep
as I drift into complacency
as I don't save the world
as I don't wait to pull my queen out
as I move my bishop erratically
across the black and white spaces

and maybe I ascend.

Maybe I am this and maybe that is okay.

Maybe it's okay to be the one who feels.

No more significant than anyone else.

A prophet of emotion.

The canary who swallowed the coal mine.

Maybe it's okay and maybe the fire is too.

Enter the Cartoon Bluebirds

oh god dammit
enter the cartoon bluebirds
enter me skipping through green fields
eyes closed turned upward to the sun
soaking in the thick mushy grossness
of love
enter the sleeplessness
enter the constant churning thoughts
of the idea that someone loves me

enter the wrecking ball of puppies
enter footie pajamas and popcorn
enter the endless tsunami of kisses
crashing over me again and again and again
drowning me in salty-awful-wonderful
exit nights spent sleeping on half of a bed
exit the bull from my china shop heart
he just floats off into the sky
like some strange giant concert blimp
exit this one brand of loneliness
let me find in its place a true fireplace sense of purpose
this red string tied to my tooth
to a door
holding me on the brittle bare soul of my truth
face squished tightly
mouth wide open
hoping
praying
that someone doesn't slam the door shut

Defenestration

I have defenestrated my friendship with a black mamba snake that would get mad at me for screaming every time that she bit me.

I have defenestrated a large number of alarm clocks with varying blaring noises. One clock was missing hours and I couldn't stand to watch it move so quickly through a single day of my life, so calloused and caustic, so of course, I defenestrated said alarm clock.

I defenestrated my scroll-length list of "things the world wants me to accomplish in my lifetime" and replaced it with a list of "things that I will work hard to make happen because they deserve to happen."

I defenestrated that rain cloud which I made from blowing smoke up my own ass and out of my mouth, as it faded into the sky like a grey balloon I realized it was never as big as I liked to think it was.

I defenestrated love that sacrificed my love instead of cultivating it.

I defenestrated cold pizza from Lil Caesar's.

I defenestrated a television set which only played one o'clock infomercials and I made a bed for my poems in its place.

(I tucked them in, read them a story, kissed them on the forehead and turned out the lights, they slept like babies.)

I defenestrated any conversation with a fellow man where they wanted to flaunt to me how shittily they treated a woman. I defenestrated a decent amount of my preconceived notions on gender roles flicking them one at a time out the window like pennies, like wishes, I defenestrated most of my identity as a man but just before letting the word *queer* slip in, I realized I'm a little too dedicated to this idea that if I hold myself to the right example maybe I can make the word *man* something that I don't feel I have to let go of.

I closed the window.

A tree branch tapped on the glass, a reminder that I still had that time machine, I could rewind it all and have it all back but I didn't.

I unleashed the lock on my window again and I threw out volume after volume of the fiction that I had written about myself, I flung titles like "Manic Pixie Dream Boy" and "Everyone I Love Will Reject Me" into the vastness below. I saw the individual ink letters of the pages scatter on the sidewalk and pour into drains and I realized they were en route to a better existence, to be rewritten in guts and glory instead of stomach and sadness.

I filled a giant bucket with gallon after gallon of the water that broke when I was pregnant with love and I realized that I no longer wish to carry anything for only nine months just to give it away to the world, I wished to use my womb as a rucksack that I would carry with me through peaks and valleys, death and uncanny. what I mean to say is some things are in fact mine and there is a difference between an excavation and a purge.

I tossed the reel tapes of an ex-lover coaching me on how to be less affectionate. I tossed her video series on how to suppress your emotions with weed and self-sacrifice. I swear to god, as soon as they were gone, the floorboards unwarped from no longer carrying the weight of her words.

I defenestrated like fifteen mirrors. My apartment was far too much like a funhouse and when I put up paintings in their place I realized that a better way to examine who you are is to curate it out onto the walls.

I tore down a couple of the walls and threw them out the window. I learned to share space with my neighbors who cooked me food. They taught me the best meals come in portions to be shared.

I defenestrated my hero complex, its cape waving in the wind.

I threw out a lot of photos upon realizing that I had carbon copies securely stored in my vault heart. I looked at a photo of my grandmother and remembered watching her memories decline. I thought maybe I'd made a mistake before I realized I write poems for the same reason she shared herself so fiercely. Because neither of us will ever disappear. Memory can transcend death.

Death became a butterfly and fluttered out the window on its own.

I defenestrated some door knobs to remind me to open up.

I defenestrated a broken teapot to remind me I don't have to scream under pressure.

I defenestrated the broken Christmas lights in my head.

And that time machine was still there, humming like a refrigerator. That time machine that said you can go back. I let it drop out the window, sounding like a baby grand piano as it hit the ground and I realized that God doesn't spend its time fixing its mistakes, it spends its time making room for new ones.

Boulder

Boulder's not racist.
Boulder has a black friend.

Boulder has skyscrapers
you just can't see them.

They're well-hidden,
the fifty story high rises
that people put Merrells on to climb
to the top of
just to look down on you.

Boulder is a Ben and Jerry's ice cream shop
but if you order the wrong flavor
you will be scolded
and asked to leave.

Boulder is having tofu tikka masala
at an authentic Indian restaurant for dinner
but Boulder is sneaking through
the KFC drive-thru
at one in the morning.

Boulder is running faster than you.

Boulder is slapping mandalas on Starbucks cups
hiding the siren and the shipwreck.

Boulder goes to poetry shows to hear itself
read to itself.

Boulder is clapping for the wrong reasons.

Boulder used its witchy manifestations
to conjure up a statute against rent control

in the eighties.

Boulder meditates in downward dog
passed out in the sundown saloon
covered in its own piss.

Boulder went to a silent retreat
and wants to talk to you about how life changing it
was.

Boulder is creating new digital technological arms
to pat itself on the back with.

Pearl Street loves us all
like a giant happy Buddha that is allergic
to cigarettes and homeless people.

Boulder doesn't have a homelessness problem,
it solved that with Longmont.

Boulder doesn't have any crime.
Just an occasional slip-up
to be addressed with a consultation
documented by your manager
addressing how terrible
your golf swing has gotten.

Boulder is getting a tarot reading from Charles Schwab.

Boulder has lots of marginalized people
nailed to the walls of its galleries.

Boulder presents Bohemian University
where for thirty k a year you can smoke cigarettes
and snap to confusing poems.

Boulder doesn't do cars—they kill the earth
and Boulder needs a ride to Denver.

Boulder's back alleys are very clean
and sponsored by local frat houses.

Boulder's back alleys smell like Bruce Banner
and pepper spray.

Boulder's back alleys sound like daddy slapping you
on the hand in a courtroom.

Boulder's back alleys taste like kombucha.

The kombucha comes in growlers.
It tastes like India Pale Ales and entitlement.

Boulder is getting a healing session for its hangover.

The hangover will not go away.

Boulder is a hangover from a ten dollar pint of dream.

Gluten-free violence.

Cage free rape culture.

Farm to table ignorance.

Boulder doesn't shower because Boulder doesn't
have to go to work.

Boulder, you have to go to work.

And the toxins are running down the 36 into Denver
and Denver is too late and I am Denver and I am Boulder
and I drove up the 36 to hear myself read to myself.

Why I Write Poetry

because
when it comes
it comes like a mack truck
and I don't have the strength
to plant my heels
firmly in the dirt
and slow it down
and I don't want it to pass on by
so my only choice
is to stick out my thumb
jump in and ride along
with this shady strung-out
truck driver
until one of us
is ready to kill the other

because
when it comes
it comes like a great woman
and I'm usually
and inconveniently
drunk
so I ask her to dance
in a loud room
where maybe she won't notice
my slurring
and I wear my cologne thick
so maybe she won't smell
the booze on my breath
and the dance never lasts long
and usually
I end up taking a cab home
and usually
she goes her own separate way
but sometimes
she comes with me

and we spend the night together
tossed in madness and revelation

because
when it comes
it comes like shock therapy
and in the pain
the swelling of the temples
the shaking of the muscles
the boiling of blood cells
sometimes
there is a moment of strong breath
where some ghost escapes
and someone else sees it
and them and me
will always have that
even if I'm not all there

because
when it comes
it comes like a letter bomb
and I could just throw it away
never open it
and the truth is
if I did that
I would be fine
but time and again
I play russian roulette
I do what's worst for me
I open the letter
I inhale the toxins
I remind myself
that I am not god
and I am reasonably sure
that god would not be who they are
if any of us
were ever considerate enough
to give them a choice
in the matter

How to Punch Yourself in the Face

It was a great day to call out of work and pace around
my bedroom punching myself in the face.
It was a great day to do some serious self-reflection
and come up with a five year plan.
Today my five year plan consisted of listening to Anne
Waldman while eating Del Taco dollar menu in my car.
Today my five year plan is to try to hold myself
accountable to shaving my head once a week,
keeping my beard trimmed, my pubes at a manageable
masculine length that says I care, but I don't care too much

and that's my truth

I do care, but I don't care too much.

Somedays I fantasize
that I am a middle-aged housewife
living in Highlands Ranch.

My reality consisting of keeping my house respectable and
providing an interesting mixed beverage
for a weekly gathering of neighborhood women
for book club
where we discuss the latest grocery store novel

but of course
secretly
we all are spending a large amount of our time
watching tentacle porn.

Today my five year plan is to punch myself repeatedly
in the face while listening to Eckhart Tolle
in the driver's seat of my car.

I tell myself I am rebuilding

that even Siddhartha Gautama had a period of denial.

I tell myself this isn't damaging, it's asceticism.

I have thrown every page of my entire catalog
of furniture out of the window;
a swift defenestration of every luxury
that once surrounded me.
The only logical next step is to begin to disband myself,
to punch myself repeatedly in the face.

And I wonder with this face in shades of blue
will I ever find my born-sexy-yesterday?
My manic pixie dream girl?
Who will accompany me to Thanksgiving dinner?
To the newest reincarnation of Batman?

My latest movie is struggling in the box office.
My latest movie is getting terrible reviews.
Maybe I wanted my latest movie to be somewhat terrible.
Maybe I wanted my latest movie to document
how much of a shit I do not give right now.
Praise be to Joaquin Phoenix.
Maybe the last thing I want is to sell out the theater.
Maybe what I really want is to not exist anymore.

Scratch that.

What I truly want is to punch myself repeatedly in the face.

It takes a lot of energy to wish *happy birthday*
to every person you've ever loved in your life.

It takes a lot of energy to water your relationships, to
provide them with appropriate levels of sunshine

and after all of that it takes a long time to disappear,
to find the right crowbar to pull up the floorboards,

to rid the crawlspace of spiders,
to somehow manage to make the wood unnoticeable
with you beneath it.

Today my five year plan is to turn down the static
on my radio head.

This is how to disappear completely.

I'm not here.
I'm floating down the Colorado River
in a shirt that says "California".
I'm trying to meditate but I'm too busy
yelling at the aspen trees for being so damn cliché.

We get it, you're golden, you're beautiful.
I get it, I'm golden, I'm beautiful.

I am the aforementioned aspen tree

but everyone turns a blind eye when this aspen tree says
something devastatingly shitty to someone during a break up.
Everyone turns a blind eye when this aspen tree didn't vote
because they didn't want to dig through their moving boxes
for their voter registration.

Maybe the aspen tree isn't gendering itself
as an aspen tree today.

Maybe the aspen tree is a fichus.

Maybe the aspen tree wants to be a green Starbucks umbrella
or a lamppost that's been struck by lightning.

Maybe the aspen tree is eating Del Taco dollar menu in his car
listening to A Tribe Called Quest
because it is hard to have a solid identity
on a planet that is rotating around the sun

at sixty-six thousand miles per hour.

I step outside into slow motion

telephone wires leaning closer to the earth each moment,

cars crashing in long languid lines,

boulders rolling slowly down mountains,

a poet on fire in a smoking jacket jumps
from his second story window,

his arms flailing as he descends in small frames per second,

the dwindling of bank accounts,

the depression of a long green electric line,

observed by ten thousand blue collared male
corporate entities,

an untrained heart pushed through esophagus,

sinking into the sour of stomach acid,

crashing with the leaves,

all on film,

all so painfully slow,

armless branches and dry rain,

eyes turned down to the ground,

I guess that's why they call it The Fall.

I am driving to Home Depot listening to We Can Work It Out. I am parking at Home Depot and leaning back my driver's seat. I am readjusting my rearview mirror. I am staring at the doorlight on the ceiling of my Kia-sponsored Soul. I am getting synthetic sunburn beneath this synthetic sun. I am evacuating my vehicle and locking the doors of perception. I am entering the store through the exit sign. I am wandering aimlessly around Home Depot. I am three hours balls deep into Home Depot and we're still not there. I am looking for enlightenment down the lamp aisle. I am comparing fifty sample shades of blue. I am calling Code Adam on my inner child. I am asking an employee if they carry dogwood. I am asking for nine inch nails. I am brought closer to god. I am running through the fire exit of Home Depot. I am stealing the wood and nails. I am driving manically to the cash register building. I am carrying my cross into the elevator. I am watching the elevator change floors like stations of the cross. I am heartbeat heartbeat heartbeat. I am assembling the cross. I am nailing my own hands to the cross. I am hanging beneath a blood moon. I have blessed myself into my own nightmare. I have birthed myself into a vacuum of distraction.

I am probably bored

and then
Eckhart Tolle lands on the roof in a rainbow hot air balloon. He slaps me across the face a solid seven times and he helps me down from my cross.

We leave it behind and go and grab milkshakes.

He drives me home and it is home and I realize this is home, the place that you cannot unshed.

The face that is revealed
when the bruises that you never needed
to give yourself
heal.

Variations on a Complaint in a Restaurant

I told the waiter that my soup was cold
and he threw it in my face and told me
I sounded just like his ex-wife.

I told the waiter that my soup was cold
and he left. He returned with a shovel
and began digging and digging through
the tile floor of the restaurant into the
dirt of the earth until he uncovered
some kindling and two good sticks which
he used to start a fire and over the fire
he heated my soup and it was love but
that strange kind of love where someone
creates a hard solution to show you the
love they have for you. I said to the waiter
that I knew he loved me before all that
noise. That I was planning to tip him well
and to tip him the same, despite all of this.

I told the waiter that my soup was cold
and the waiter said no, the soup isn't cold
you are just eating the soup at the wrong
time and I said fine then I'll go back and
eat the soup when you're not working.

I told the waiter that my soup was cold
and he sat down beside me, grabbed my
spoon and tasted it. Then he tasted it again
and again and again until he'd eaten the
whole bowl of soup and then I looked him
in his kind full eyes and we both opened
our mouths and said "compersion" in the
same song at the same moment.

I told the waiter that my soup was cold
and the waiter told me that he had just
been to the doctor and the doctor told
him that he had a degenerative disease
and that his days alive on this planet were
numbered and I told the waiter that the
soup is fine. It's fine. It's fine.

I told the waiter that my soup was cold
but it wasn't. He took the soup to the
back and brought me out a fresh bowl
of warm soup, he apologized profusely
for the inconvenience and I sat and
waited alone in the steam of my deceit
for the soup to cool so that I could drink
it.

I told the waiter that my soup was cold
and across the table Matt Clifford shook
his head at me and said no no no no no
the soup isn't cold, you are too warm for
the soup. Have you ever thought that a
sloth doesn't see itself as slow moving
but rather revels in the joy that the world
is moving so beautifully fast around it?
No you only think about yourself,
said Matt Clifford.

I told the waiter that my soup was cold
so he picked up the soup and threw it
like a professional baseball fast pitch
against the wall and then his eyes all
kerosene and lit matchstick he yelled
"Anger is a secondary emotion!" and I
told him that doesn't bring my soup back.

I told the waiter that my soup was cold

and I realized I was the waiter and that
the soup was cold and I had been just
staring and staring at this poor customer
for an eternity as they starved in my
section which I had most definitely
neglected to properly take care of.

I told the waiter that my soup was cold.
I told myself that I deserved a better mirror.

I told the truth in almost all of my bodies.

I'm in all of these restaurants
and the soup is always god damn cold.

The Inbetween

This right here
is The Inbetween.

The space we create not by pushing out music notes
in hopes of getting rest
but three thousand miles of Nothing, Kansas.

I am a fidgety person.
There are home videos of me as a child
pulling out toy after toy after toy to the front lawn
endlessly bringing every plastic gift
to the attention of my mother
behind a video camera.

I have never done this to say
"this is mine,"

but rather to say
"this can be ours,"

but now the last scraps of my childhood
have been dragged to the hot lawn
and I find myself sitting in an empty room
beneath a broken ceiling fan.
I find myself in The Inbetween.

When faced with limbo,
it is natural to want to make one's self small.

This only makes sense

but please take a minute to believe me when I say
there is no power in not feeding yourself.

Malnutrition is sometimes a symptom of you believing

that you do not deserve your space in the world.

You deserve your space in the world.
Just remember
you do not have to swallow anyone else to claim it.

My heart tells me to turn back,
that home is in the rearview mirror
and there's some truth to that
but what you'll find when you arrive
broken-toed at your childhood home
is that the rooms are much smaller than you remember

so I keep walking
when the vacancy signs in the eyes of strangers
are as jagged as the letter N and as full as the letter O
I keep walking
and at night I sleep
by which I mean I guess I close my eyes.

I pray
but when God stops listening
my prayers start to feel like throwing paper planes
at a brick wall
and maybe that's The Inbetween.

I am writing incredibly long love letters
with large spaces for names and dates
and I hold out believing
that the empty rooms in these poems
are just on hold
reserved for the right immaculate moment.

A Self-Analysis

Some days I leave my arms at home
to give other people the chance to show me
how to conduct a symphony.

I am an owl in many ways
but most of all in the way I like to be alone at night
staring out my window
sitting on my tree branch
waiting for the field mice to come to me.

When I look at the hairs on my legs
I see thousands of tiny trees and I think about
the day each seed was planted.
I think about the way I am so very large
because I am one billion things so small.

I have a hard time with spiders
because I don't want to kill them and
I know that I am ultimately unimportant to them
but I feel them crawling up my leg in bed
and when I look they're never there
but my vulnerability is sometimes counter-intuitive
to my survival instinct
there is a certain amount of acceptance of death
that comes along with trust.

I refill ice trays in the freezer like a madman
like some great fleshy robot filled
with a singular algorithm to make sure there is never
one moment where this house will be without ice.

I don't drink enough water.

In the middle of the twilight I talk to ghosts.
They carry all these stories about regret and war

and I'm just trying to sing myself
to sleep with songs of faith and renewal
but they clean their guns on the edge of my bed
and sometimes I like to swim
on top of their uneasy oceans.

I papercut my finger
on my contract to myself
and when the blood begins to run
I put it beneath the cold water faucet
and watch as it pours down the drain
and sometimes the water rises
and the sink fills up and the bathroom floods
until I'm underwater in my apartment
scuttling along like a crab
on the warped wood floor
but I do not drown, I sleep best in rip tide.
I dance in disaster.

Sometimes I fall asleep to radio static.
There is a room so quiet you can hear your blood
in your veins and the silence will drive you mad they say.
I talk so loud about how good I am at silence.
How American it is to always know what to say
and that's the thing.

I think I'm an auditory citizen of the world until it gets quiet
and I can hear the national anthem reminder
that I don't know how to sight read a page of rest symbols.

I dance like I am protesting dancing,
Like if I flail my arms enough they'll call it satire.

When I dance with women I follow their hips
and pretend I am so keen to the difference between
control and influence.

Sometimes I get stuck in the middle of a poem

and I don't know how to end it.
Sometimes I'll get real cute
and just throw out a one-liner like something
Oscar Wilde would say at a cocktail party
but sometimes I'll just take a minute to be in it.
I'll walk around the poem like an empty apartment
opening the closets looking for clues about
the person who lived here before
and sometimes I'll find that there's nothing but
wire hangers in the closet
or sometimes I'll run out screaming
chased by skeletons

not tonight.

The Tilt in the Axis of the Earth

but one boy dared to go play in traffic
and despite what you might picture for him
the traffic learned to swerve around his magic.
From the sidelines the other boys looked onward
and they saw illusion.

It wasn't illusion.
It was a victory of the soul.
Stubborn thumping rebellion outweighing cold measured logic

the tilt in the axis of the earth.

Broken-Winged Bird

In China, they built a glass bridge where people can walk out and stare straight down to the bottom of a giant canyon, three thousand feet below. They say that several times a day, tourists will walk out to the middle of the bridge and become stunned when they look straight down at the vastness below them. They will freeze, unable to move, some have delusions that they are about to fall. This is me right now. I have stepped out onto the bridge and how bravely I took step after step to the center of the canyon, but now I've looked down, and I have seen the face of God and He wasn't smiling. No, She wasn't smiling at all. In fact, They were looking back at me less like a parent and more like someone across the room. That moment no one talks about. The conversations between you and an acquaintance you'll never make acquaintance with. That is God, and it is paralyzing. To realize that the vastness is not still. It's moving and rapidly. Bugs crawling under rocks, boulders chucking themselves into rolling rivers, shadows of birds swinging through pompously blocking a small cell of sunlight. It's a lot to realize. To realize you may be 3,000 feet suspended in the air but if you stand too long, if you stare too long, you might think you're falling, and if you stare longer yet, you might just be. Caught by nothing but wind and the music of this stomach drop. A punch to the inside of your heart. The realization that the wings of the stage have taken off, they've taken your coat, your hat, your cane and all you have now is the stage. You hold tightly onto your microphone until that too is taken away and all that remains of every pixelated cell of your sturdy footing is you.

It is you and every set of eyes ever. The eyes of your mother. The eyes of the great judge. The eyes of critics. The eyes of time, of death, of sweetness, of morning breath, of every cancer, every sun and moon, the eyes of a sideways love half buried in your pillows, or at least the potential of one.

And something whispers in your ear "speak" but you don't.
Your lungs have been replaced with coarse bags of sand and
your heart is a hot air balloon, weaning off of propane.
Your heart is a blue flame in a red world, and so you crank
it. You slowly twist the knob and let loose an evensong for
a chorus of morning ears. You let loose eulogy for pain.
You let free the broken-winged bird you never knew you
swallowed. If you're lucky. And in the moment of deafening
applause you hear nothing. You are not there. You're floating
over the bridge still, you're consumed by the overwhelming
identity of existence. You feel. If you're one of the lucky ones.
And when it resumes, the people blur like shaken up film,
the days are moonless nights, the moons are sunless days.

It's somehow shrunken and expansive.
Your blue flame becomes you.
The red world turns to your distinct shade of blue.
This is not sadness. This is not some painting.
It's much more, and it's incredible really.
The glass cracks just a little,
and there looking down on the vastness,
and elsewhere as you finish the last line
of your best poem
you realize,

this is not the holy moment.

They all are.

That One Week Where I Thought I Had The Death Disease

There was that one week
where I thought I had the death disease.
I put quarters in every gumball machine
and I chewed so many gumballs.
I threw pies at all the assholes I knew.

In some strange twist of events
I still found myself brushing my teeth well.
You'd think there'd be a resolve but no
I still found myself valuing brushing my teeth.
I also began making my bed
maybe because I thought to myself
well, I've got this death disease and my days are numbered.

I deserved all sorts of things that week.
Twenty-minute breaks at work where I'd just wander
to other floors in the building
pacing like a mindless patient in a hospital
through other people's drudgery.
I'd wink at strange men
sitting at their desk just trying to feed themselves.

I stared out the corporate window at the Rocky Mountains
and I tried to capture frames of them
blinking erratically
as if the optic nerve were a classic polaroid camera;
the green foothills, the brown mountains, the white snowcaps
like God saying *fuck you, my tiramisu is better than yours*
like God saying *fuck you, I love you this much*
and realizing that every person in my life loves me that much.

I used my water cup for soda at Tokyo Joe's.
I didn't feel any shame.
I stared the assistant manager right in his patchy bearded face

as I slurped down Dr. Pepper like it was the classiest wine.
I looked at him in his eyes and I saw myself.
I realized I was the assistant manager at Tokyo Joe's.
Even in the nucleus of my death dance
I didn't quite know how to be.

I wasn't a communist insurgent
overthrowing the capitalist structure of the world
of the everything.

I wasn't death riding in on a pale horse.

I simply remained me.
My lymph nodes swollen like small galaxy.

This didn't allow me access to the manual on how to universe.

It seems it takes time and space and patience to universe.
It seems to me that communion with everything
is more of a goal than a possibility.
It is still a good goal to have,
I thought, as I finished my sample of Dr. Pepper,

as I walked out onto the median of the road,
as I straddled the double yellow line of matter,
as I realized that it seems to me
I put way too much energy into things,
like defiance, or worse yet, self-destruction
as a means to matter.

That this is probably not the way to remain a child
that as ugly as responsibility may seem
as much as we want to believe we are babies in oversized suits
the truth is we are animal-skinned drums
never truly exploring the echoes
of our sounds unto ourselves
too fascinated by the big room

to dig deep into the small big room,
the one that paces its cage
in the haunted marrow
of our bones.

Believing I had the death disease,
all that was revealed to me was the mirror of what I wasn't,
all that was revealed to me was gratitude,
buckets and buckets of gratitude.
My eyes broke down in temper tantrums of gratitude,
lying on my bed in antibiotics.

I began crying thinking about the way
I tried to ring you out of your love

and I promise you this, poem,
I will stop trying to weigh love in grams.

Believing I had the death disease,
I spoke frankly each and every day
to my mother and father
on the phone,

who still reminded me I haven't paid my toll fees
who said yeah you just can't think about it
and I said *okay good luck to me with that*
and they said *no no no you'll get it*
and I said *ok*

and all of the phones on this floor
kept ringing and ringing
so i just kept saying ok
ok.

The Apple Store

I walked into the apple store and asked the man if I could buy an apple.

He told me no.

I said that isn't fair.

I want to buy an apple.

He said to me "well, I don't want to sell you an apple."

At this point, another someone walked by and the man gave them an apple.

"Well, just give me the apple," I said to the man.

"No," he said again.

"Why?" I said.

"Why not?" he said.

"I'm hungry," I said to him.

"You should work on not being hungry," he said to me.

"That's precisely what I'm trying to do," I said to him.

"No," he said, "you're trying to be full."

"Same thing," I said.

"Not at all," he said.

"I want to speak to the manager," I said to the man.

"I am the manager," the man said.

"Well then, I want to speak to your boss," I said.

"I am my own boss," he said.

"You can't be your own boss," I said.

"Yes, you can," he said, "you would understand that if you weren't so hungry."

"Well, I'm going to be hungry until you give me that apple," I said.

"I guess you'll always be hungry," he said, slowly biting into the apple.

Bus Stop Koan

I sat one day, impatiently waiting for the bus. There was snow everywhere, and the bus stop was empty except for one man with a long beard, bundled up heavily. I made eye contact with him and he in return with me, though neither of us spoke a word to one another. Taking a seat beside him, I looked out at the streets and buildings, all drowned out in white snow. There was a silence between us when the man began to very loudly say "Ring ring! Ring ring!" then again silence. I thought of this as a one-time thing, until several minutes later when the man again said "Ring ring! Ring ring!" I looked at him to assess his well-being but said nothing.

Again – "Ring ring! Ring ring! Ring ring!"

"Hello?" I said.

"Oh, hello," he said smiling, "how are you today?"

Dear Human,

I might eat you.

You really don't have much control over it.

If I am not the monster that eats you
it will most likely be another.

Perhaps the great alligators in the sewers of Denver
perhaps the green-eyed mountain monster of Bailey
perhaps the monster of indecision
of anxiety, of restlessness, of slow heartbreak,

but right now I am not hungry
and it would mean a lot to me if you would sit with me
and hold my hand.

It's been so long since someone's held me
and part of me believes
that it's not my only purpose to eat you
that maybe the men with pitchforks have boxed me in.

In short,
there's no guarantees that I won't eat you
but I promise you if you stay with me right now
I will do my best to love you.

Hero

I watch like a child
the way that you take your thumb
to the timber line
and erase houses
like a prayer
that we all return into the heart
of the Earth.

I never thought I'd breathe anything so deeply
as the ashes of you that you so easily left to the wind.

Kissing
the black ink
of the skull
that graces your neck
I have learned
how holiness is something
that can never be contained in bibles.

You break from dark lineage into a round world waiting.
You and I know you exist in every space in every moment

and no space more apparently to my song
than the caverns in my heart that I had no idea
contained amazing amounts
of white quartz and amethyst
until you blew away the wreckage

left me drowning in a thousand lifetimes of tears
that I've carried for lifetimes.
I take to sea in a rowboat with the holy ghost of you
and in the tempest that you extract from me

like planets all with different gravities
carved with runes and promises

and maybe I'm lucky enough to cry
to the very bottom of this wind-up bird wishing well

and maybe I'm lucky enough to bless you
with the ones that fall on your chest.

Maybe I'm lucky enough to dance with you
down empty streets in valleys
among the kamikaze rain drops
that don't even penetrate my skin.

In your grandfather's paint-stained flannel
I am immune to anything that would try to hurt me.

In the onyx core of your white bed sheets
I am so perfectly unamerican,
unnamed, undecided.

You tell me that I am a cathedral inside of a cathedral
and I need you to know that having seen you rise
through giant mounds of heartache
that you are the fucking sun illuminating
every single one

of my stain-glassed windows
as I die in a fire
of every color

with
you.

Sound Reverberated Off of Mountains

I swallowed the city
before the city could swallow me.

In anticipation of the haunted smog
which rolls along like mustangs
into the last solid chamber of my America.

I watched a dream die.
A dream of big thoughts
like lightning bolts,
large and unsustainable,
filling the last pixelated square of
unlit wanderlust.

And in the unlit wanderlust
I learned to walk by sound.
I learned to move
by the layered truths of reality
and I learned to love
what I have not yet seen
but that which I truly believe
exists.

I swallowed the city
inward like two aspirin tablets
past the vacuum of the spaces
between my sweet teeth
onward in rivers to the pit of me.

I felt the brick walls falling
in the canyons of me
like sixty-seven thousand soup cans falling down
endless flights of stairs.

And inside of me there are

endless flights of stairs and
each day I ask myself if I am
going to walk downward into
them or if I am going to climb
up them and I know they
might be the same thing except
that's not true at all and
each flight of stairs very
well goes to very different
places.

The city attempted to swallow
me in its placebo fever of death
and I yelled deep, deep into the
belly of the city as to make it
bounce back against the
mountains in hopes of
disorienting the city that I loved
into possibly thinking it was and is
hearing the voice of God.

Because we all are and I can't
argue with you about that of which
I am certain. That my God is a
God of sound reverberating off
mountains and I push it right
back against it until I hear a
full-mantled chorus of every
fire and every flood in my
wet, hot life.

I think about the way that we
give birth is in every way. I think
about the way we father our
poems and days and then we
let them go.

I drown in sweaty, undying brows
of om dripping with the hard work
of a soul in its best sunlight.

I still plant seeds for later.

I swallowed the city and from
my belly the city grew
for me. It grew for me because
I wanted it to grow for me.

I still plant seeds for later.

For the day the ocean grows
sick of our bee sting and swats
back at us.

I plant seeds for when this world
is sick of shooting at itself.

For dreams that I dare say already
exist because I was there in them
and you and you and you were there.

Bar Rhapsody

A man walks into a bar, says to the bartender "oh man, bartender, I have had the worst day of my life and all I want is a drink." The bartender says "I can get you a drink but let me tell you this. I have just returned from a deep, dark spiritual pilgrimage wherein I meandered the webs of collective consciousness and I have had a striking vision that should you ingest any drink here tonight that what you will do is continue to perpetuate your reliance on alcohol to self-medicate as an alternative to valuable introspective work you could be doing. There is also an irony that it is alcohol that so often depresses you, keeps you unhealthy, negatively influences your decisions and ultimately imprisons you. It is your savior that is also your destruction. Do you not see this? It is your savior that is also your destruction." The man thinks for a minute before saying, "yeah, but you're a bartender, so I guess that basically means you're the devil, and I'll have a Coors Light."

A man runs into a bar and keeps running and keeps running until he clears the bar and runs out the backdoor and into the night to find countless other late night establishments to run through if for nothing else, just the pure joy of being an awakening blip of a story on the road map of the stranger who turns to their buddy and says "did that man just run through the bar?"

A woman walks into a bar and orders a drink, she slowly sips her drink, pays her tab, thanks the bartender and heads home for a good night's rest. A lot of women just really have their shit together and don't need to make a drama of everything.

A monkey walks into a bar and orders a Tom Collins in monkey talk. The bartender returns with a Gin and Tonic and the monkey, again in monkey talk, kindly yet assertively tells the bartender that this is not the drink he ordered. The bartender once again incorrectly understands the monkey and thinks that the monkey is stating that there is an inherent value in removing the tariffs on trade that Donald Trump has issued and the bartender says he doesn't disagree before moving on to tend to his other customers. The monkey is understandably upset, and begins to devise a plan not for a device that translates monkey talk to English, but rather translates English to monkey talk because the monkey is well-educated and understands that there is an ethnocentric belief that we must adapt to the existing culture when in fact there are incredible benefits to considering the value of cultural anomalies on shifting the structure of society as we know it.

A man walks into a bar and sits down next to another man. He is instantly struck by the unspoken romantic connection he is experiencing with this other man but doesn't say anything. The silent man recently went through a breakup and doesn't feel he has the capacity for much human interaction in general, let alone to offer his heart up to someone new. The other man stirs his drink, furious at the gods for cursing him with the ability to hear other people's thoughts, as the heartbreak of knowing what goes unsaid is time and time again unbearable.

A bear walks into a bar. Patrons of the bar run out the back door, duck under counters and some call the local animal rescue. The bear is devastated. He had spent the majority of the day getting up the courage to interact with humans, reassuring himself that he is more than just a monster in their eyes, and finding this to be false the bear wanders off into the night. He doesn't give up though. He decides first thing in the morning he will begin to play guitar and he will make it his mission to tour the world playing songs on his lovely guitar until he becomes an inarguable fixture in the movement for bears to be seen as gentle, creative creatures, and so much more than the monsters they're portrayed as.

A woman walks into a bar one afternoon and orders an Old-Fashioned from the bartender. The bartender tells the woman that he is new and has never made an old-fashioned before. The woman reassures the bartender that she is sure it will be fine and the bartender pulls bitters, prepares his orange peel, and grabs a nice whiskey to begin prepping the drink. The bartender hands the woman her drink and tells her to be honest. The woman tries the drink and it is terrible. The balance is off and she can barely stomach the taste of it with each sip, but she looks at the bartender in his eyes and she is struck by how badly he wants the drink to be good. She thinks logically she should be honest. The bartender did say he is new and to give him the truth, but she strangely feels pulled the opposite direction. "It's delicious," she says and the bartender smirks and says, "thank you." Later that night, the woman can't sleep so she calls the bar. She detects from the voice that the man answering the phone is the bartender and she tells him the truth, that the drink was terrible. She thinks this was all very uncomfortable and even possibly excessive, but it was right. What I did was right. She sleeps like a newborn baby.

A powerful genie floats into a bar and sits down at a seat in the corner and cries deeply. Everyone at the bar is somewhat disoriented by this blue phantasm weeping as they are trying to enjoy their drinks until one person approaches him and asks what is wrong. The genie says that everywhere he goes, everyone takes from him. Takes and takes. That he has found himself in a life where his only purpose is to grant the wishes of others. One guy at the bar says, "not tonight, Genie," and the people of the bar all cheers in agreement. "Whatever you want tonight, Genie, we will provide it for you." All night long the genie is granted free drinks and hugs and intimate conversations where for the first time in his life he was more than just what the world told him he is.

My ego walks into a bar and the bar is flooded, overwhelmingly flooded with the thick black waters of relationship drama and complaints about me not having enough time and conversations that I elevate to critical levels over things that probably could have been quick asides. The poor customers of the bar learn to live under these overwhelming egoic conditions until finally I do some self-work and the ego fizzles down. The floors are still a little wet, but at least there's breathing room and at least I'm trying. At least I'm trying.

A man walks into a bar and holds up a space gun. He says, "with this space gun, I can complete rework the rules of language as we know it!" He fires the space gun and the bar is swept up in a green of hue light. Some nothing difference delivered unto this this. Depiction, some oracular, crevices within minds, abandoned we wonder elevation? Best the best we may be unsure we rethink. Delivered into something new delivered into us. Gun fired pew pew pew and then we return to the way things were before then, but things will never be the way they were before because we are all forever changed in every moment and I've been realizing this a lot lately. I dealt with what for me was a very difficult circumstance. A circumstance wherein I fell deeply in love with a woman and she fell deeply in love with me, and we allowed ourselves to do so, despite being in very different places in our lives and wanting different things, and I've spent the majority of the last few months trying to figure out how best to love this person before realizing I needed to let her go. Through all of this, I saw our love as something unique. Some circumstance that had never before happened, and the truth is every love is so fucking big, but this situation was not unique. There is no lack of love. My identity of love is it is the very fiber of everything that we are. I can sincerely say that I love every person in every one of these hypothetical bars. I can honestly say I love you, even if I hate you. The only danger is apathy and I am not an apathetic person. I'm a writer, and I'm trying to say something, and I think what I'm trying to say, or do, is use these random bar scenarios to uncover aspects of my feelings about life, and they feel like math equations. I feel thrown into the circumstances of these fictional bars and I find myself caring what happens. There is a variety of experiences out there waiting for you, and there is no such thing as not reacting to them. What I'm saying is I don't regret. What I'm saying is it is all insightful. It has all been said. Don't try so hard to be original that you forget to be yourself. Thank you.

Clone

If I could,
I would clone myself
and leave me with you.
I would still walk away
but also I would stay
and water the pots in your garden
and feed the soil of your little girls' sunlight
while I sat here away from you too
writing poetry about you
and I can't be too sure
that when the winter came again
I would not leave again
finding myself writing perfect poems
about how perfectly
I would have loved you.

Bukowski, again

oh holy poetic father
your long skinny soul
scrawled across the backs
of thousands of naked spines
and how each drop
of battery acid
dripped from the dots
in the eyes
and the holy crosses
across the t's
that hung suspended in time
to reach out like
hands with holes
just to barfight my liver
just to curbstomp my stomach
into submission
has helped me sift through
the madness for the word, the
line, the way
but here we are
at the end of the way
and the bottle wasn't bottomless
I've seen the bottle
dropped off the building
and smashing against reality
a fist of misogyny
an inability to step away
from the drunken typewriter
to never grow
(as did the flowers you loathed)

there are too many great poets
who pot shot the page nightly
but never stepped out
of the square ring

to see the round earth desperate
for a pair of rugged hands
to build the cities they dreamed up

in their dreams unrealized
unrealized dreams are the worst nightmares
and Bukowski
sweet devil Bukowski
you are the worst nightmare

the victim flower that cursed the fiery sun
for trying to keep him alive

Snippet of a Man Talking About His New Television Set

So, I was walking around the store, just out grabbing a few things for the house and I just happened to wander into the electronics department and there she was. I'd always heard you can get some good deals on TVs after the Super Bowl but I never thought it would be this good. I won't tell you how much I paid but I will tell you this - a 60-incher like this usually goes for a couple k. I asked the guy at the store about it. Todd, I think his name was. Todd. Yeah, anyways. Super nice kid. Said it was 1080p and that I was lucky I came in when I did because it was the last one. This is actually the store model, but Todd said he'd take it down for me.

Look at that picture, am I right? makes you feel like you're at the game. the kids love it. With their video games and stuff, the graphics are just great. Also, we put the old TV down in the basement so they're pretty thrilled about that. Plus Barbara spent so much money on this nice entertainment center, I felt like we deserved a good TV to go along with it. Anyways, yeah, so I went to ring up with Todd and he got me this HDMI cable that's supposed to up the picture quality like 10% or something. I wasn't sold at first, but he said it was definitely worth it, especially with how quickly technology changes. Hard to keep up, I guess. I got the two-year warranty. Thirty bucks, but you can't be too safe. What's an extra 30 bucks for peace of mind, I say. But yeah, took her home, super easy set up. It's just nice, ya know?

The Eight of Swords

You keep handing me this crying baby like it belongs to me
and i think what I'm finding is you are a broken boat.
I think it's time I tell you I can be a river but not an ocean.
You keep asking me to sing in keys my sore voice can't reach.
I'm not a singer, I'm not a dancer, I simply bleed blood
and usually I'm searching for a sponge to clean that up
so take back this crying child that's screaming your name.

It's not mine.

I know there's blood all over my hands
but I'm not going to paint us red with it.

I'm resolved to stay in this forest for a while.
I'm resolved to sleep in tiny beds
but it's three in the morning and my eyes are fire.
I can't even hear your howls anymore.
I can't use my broken hands to dig for bones in your backyard.

I see the cage around you and I see the open door.
I'm not going to slam it shut.
I'm not going.

I've counted my own doors and left them open.
I've counted my own doors and understand that these rooms
are just compartments of one swollen heart.

I'm staying home
where it's home and I know how many doors there are.

Open your doors and carry your child
before it carries you.

We Could Fall in Love in Reverse

We could fall in love in reverse.

In the end,
I would walk around the cultural exhibits of the art museum
studying the anthropology of ghosts, of buried civilizations,
of some strange memory that I'm not so certain ever happened.
You would be a shamanic healer now,
crawling around the crawl spaces of the ethos, of your mind,
pulling at the metal cord of light switches.
You would be so vast and beautiful on your own there.

I would leave the museum,
retracing my steps back into my bed to cry
to erase words off a page.

You would turn off the lights in all the rooms
and say whatever "let's brighten this place up a bit,"
is in reverse
which would probably sound a lot
like walking in the woods with you at night.

You would cry too
tears dried up like western rivers
back into the beds of your eyes
and stir your tea the wrong way
counterclockwise.

I'd unsend that digital carrier pigeon
with its little bag of arsenic and note
"eat this or love me differently."

You'd pick up the phone
and see it's me and not answer
and that would look about the same.

We'd fight backwards
and I'm realizing just now
that I'm not so sure that peace
is the sound of screaming
sucked backed into our lungs.

I'd pull broken dishes
away from walls and hold them in my hands.
I'd untake your plate
we'd uneat dinner
we'd undrink wine
we'd uncook fake meat
and freeze it back to its home
on the fake meat farm.

I'd kiss you.
Our tongues would dance into irrelevance
of dominance versus submission
convoluted by the confusion of which way we're headed
in the mix of the kiss
I'd be almost certain we were loving in forward motion again
because it's still just us taking turns at driving.

We'd pack up the groceries
back into recyclable tote bags and collectively bring them
to the womb of the car.

I'd look at you kind of sadly on the drive home
to the grocery store
watching the sun rise in the evening.

You'd unhold my hand.

I'd scratch the back of your head
until I felt the desire to touch you
when I'd stop.

The previous afternoon we'll make the bed with our sex.

I'll uncook you lunch because I want you to stay.

I'll dance with you to no music
which still sounds the same
it still sounds the same
I still sound the same
and I'll ask you
what it would look like to never have met me
and you won't hear me
and I'll tell you how my day was
and you'll ask me how my day was
and you'll tell me how your day was
and I'll ask you how your day was
and then nothing will be said.

One morning I'll watch you fall fast awake
and in the evening you'll tell me that you know you love me
and I will tell you that I think I'm in love with you.

We'll talk every day
and I'll invite you to my cousin's unwedding
where they uncut the cake
where everyone is dancing before they make their vows
where we vow to never get married
and laugh.
We laugh and laugh

I'll blow fire into your candles
until the wax builds up.

We'll talk a couple times a week.

We'll get to unknow one another.

Kissing you by the train tracks
worried that it had crashed into us.

Walking you home
where you hand me flowers
and close the door on me

and you say you'd love to go out sometime
and I ask you if you'd like to go out sometime

and I call you
and you give me your number

and I know that you'll be someone special to me
I see you across the room and walk over to say hello

In the beginning

And in The Red Corner of This Here Life

Alright, kid.
You got hit pretty damn hard
but this shit don't stop.

This ain't the
Holiday Fuckin Inn.

I need you to
brush that dust off
your shoulders,
wipe that blood from
yer cheek,
and remind us all
why you're the champ.

It's not how hard
you can hit
it's how hard you can
get hit

so pick yer heart up
off the floor
and put that shit
right back into yer chest.

There are kids
who would die to be here
sweating under these lights.

Don't do it for me.
Don't do it for the glory.
Do it because it's what you
were born to do.

Your vocation

is tooth n nail

and yeah
it's gonna hurt.

It's gonna hurt real bad.
Yer gonna sting in places
you'd never known
but at the end of the night

you can lay down beside her

and push yer fingers
through her soft hair

and that glimmer in her eyes.

Yeah, that glimmer.

It's the only two stars you'll want
in your sky

and at the end of the
long long long long day
you can rest
like yer broken ass
has never rested before.

Heaven

He closed his eyes
as he entered onto the train
and found that the train he'd waited for
his entire life
was leaving exactly that place
where he'd thought he was headed.

How To Be Alive

Gently place two warm fingers against your neck.

Take in breath like you're loading a rucksack.

Let out breath like you're filling the entire sky.

Understand that you are filled with blood.

Understand that blood does not like to stand still.

This is how to make your blood stand still:

watch the cars roll by at forty miles per hour

realize you are not moving

but to them you roll by

at forty miles per hour.

Clench your fingers into fist and understand the strength of womb, of rosebud.

Open your fingers to the sun and understand that to grow best you have to expose frail petals to fire.

Open mouth kiss the sky.

Somewhere you are passing through the thoughts of clouds.

Somewhere they are letting you go.

You are still full of blood.

You are not this body, but this body wants you to hold it.

Often unbeknownst to us, the lungs hold the rib cage.

Muscles hold the stomach.

Our arms are left empty to hold what they will.

White blood cells rush in like firemen to fight what's burning.

They listen for where the smoke sings.

The mind makes dreams from reality.

The hands make reality from dreams.

Our mouths let lying dogs sleep.

Our bodies tell the truth.

We move forward in defiance of gravity.

The trees wave in applause.

We swallow pain, we process sorrow.

We let go of what doesn't serve us.

You are still full of blood.

The heart pushes and pulls.

The heart gives what it takes.

The heart is what dies.

Not us.

Shave Your Beard And Go Home, Sam

Shave your beard and go home, Sam.
There's no more light in this lightless room.
There's no more weight left to put on this heavy story.
You're not this room made smaller and smaller.
You're not this dance done into the point of exhaustion.
You are in fact Marin County and the faceless trees
the roadless highways, the elation at every other star
the differed sense of self that you chase after at the nose
of your undying headlights in the California night
The hidden stitching on each and every book you've ever read.

Shave your beard and go home, Sam.
You are a wild bird in an opened cage.
You are dragging around barbed wire for too many miles.
Kiss clean the past and let it disappear into the deep end of it all.
Take this baby deer into the field and shoot it in the head.
That gun will sound louder than any shouting match in history
but in history it will disappear from profanity into grace.

Shave your beard and go home, Sam.

Dear Audience,

I am sorry to say the poet will not be joining us this evening.

At the price of your disappointment
the poet has opted to delve into a search for a new truth.

The poet would like to acknowledge the hurt that this may
have afflicted onto you.

The poet understands you have seen their love
and desire their love
and want to celebrate their love.

Unfortunately, tonight,
the poet wants you to know they cannot see their love.

They cannot celebrate their love.

The poet has disappeared,
and they kindly ask that at some point

you do the same.

Unlistened-To Voicemails

As a side effect of modern convenience
I leave my voicemails unlistened to.

There is a shiny green circle
that reminds me that someone at a very specific
Mountain Standard Time loved me enough
to speak thoughts into a handheld device
in dedication to an undecided future moment
when I should resign my will to the experience
of traveling back in time to the voice
perhaps of a lover telling me that they miss me
and that they are excited to see me tomorrow night.

Or perhaps the strange, strange, strange love
of a telemarketer who clearly wants nothing more
than to let me know that I, amongst the many many
snowflakes falling from their randodialer sky
have won a fantastic five day six night cruise
to the eastern shores of some island I've never heard of
where I will go and be, probably alone, isolated to the waves
and the crisp sweet slow death of an alcoholic beverage.

On this island that they offer me on voicemail
I will not be here missing you so immensely
retracing the steps that led up to me calling you off.
I don't like the way in my darkest moments of love
I find myself so much like an army colonel
signaling the retreat of your tiny women with bayonets
on a thousand white horses that seem to always fight
for me and for our love

even if that love at times is painstakingly difficult.

I want to call off our love like a veteran surgeon
properly masked and addressed with latex gloves

cutting a delicate and mindful incision into the portion
of the body where the toxins reside and therein
I will aim not to send the anesthetized patient
into a deep state of shock but instead
simply isolate the section of the trauma
and carefully remove it and discard of it
in a perfect stainless steel container I've set aside
in anticipation of this holy moment

and then returning to the incision I've left in our love
stitching back in perfect stitches that will in time fade
until what once might have carried the weight
of every last bubbling red ounce of our romance becomes
nothing but a scar and a story that we laugh at.
I suppose that I could listen
to the voicemails that flood my inbox
in their moment of arrival;

let life flood over me like the blood from the elevator
in that one scene in The Shining
and I left stunned like the little boy in The Shining
lost to the unspoken ghosts which constantly hum
their battle cries into every unspoken-for speck of air
around us.

I suppose I could let them come as they do
but there is something to be said here about art
and control and patience
but honestly, I'm not sure that I know what it is
and honestly, I always always want nothing more
than to be so in love that I don't question
the incredibly idiotic things that I do.

Love Poem for Everything
Thank you to Ted Vaca for allowing the adapted use of his phrase "Queen City of the Plains"

When I can't stay inside my own head
let alone this half-haunted apartment.

When I bust down the door into space.

When I lie in the middle of the busy road.

When I turn my head up to the night sky
and I let it consume me.

Car honks.
The distant hum of punk rock
diving out of bars.
The sound of stale beer
on the floor
warped wood panels
some guy trash-talking
football punchy soapbox manifestos
floating down streams of consciousness.

Fingers snapping like they're trying to start a fire
the only thing getting laid is bricks.

Underground and anarchist bookstores
dreaming of 90s children's television shows
dreaming of 60s communism parties
and why shouldn't they?

The flag is torn in decades it's only pieced back together in time.

Jills in jackboots
souls in shoes
transient life in constant hearts

sheep in wolves clothing
Hawaiian shirts at funerals
crowded buses on their 36 hustle
taking the elitist drunks to
The People's Republic of Boulder

taking trustafarians to Denver,
Queen City of the Cranes
the dying hunt for empanadas for streetlights
dripping with light
closing their eyes at 2 am
but not tired.

For the devil's curly hair!
Patrolling Cap Hill at 3 am for a pulse
singing improv ethereal gutter moon chainsaw garage dumpster
surf punk to the dead trees
we made this whole thing up!

For the queen bitches on Mars
revealing armor in striptease, in unwavering loud truth
vulvas slapped like stickers on masculine walls
calling not for destruction
but reminding the Bukowskis it's getting dark outside
you'd better let your bluebird free.

For eyes in round glasses
sporadic jolts of childhood boom snap clap nursery rhymes
driving cow towns over moons and potato anthems stories
reminders that this here is what we have
and what we have is the space to be, still
that there is value in alleys that live between banks and bars

like breaths in Gibson.

Guitars still being played
marches, rallies, protests, strikes, riots
all still being played

Dylan still being played
paint slapped on shirts on sweaters
and when they ask "what does it mean?" we'll say
good question.

and when they ask "what does it mean?" we'll say
be patient, they'll figure it out someday.

Outside the window
there are metric tons of humanity
crashing against each other
like two oceans thrown together
swallowing entire continents.

Our children will eat our mistakes
like Breakfast of Champions
their poetry will be lethal to hate.

as we begin to shrink back into the Earth
we will know to look up to them.

Our children will never trip on a phone cord.

They will grow flowers in the plots of our graves.

They will sing in octaves that we've never heard.

They won't know industry
or need
they won't need to

my hope is
they will bloom organic
in houses made of opened blood cells.

Our children will shine
and cheers with love potions.
They will see through owl's eyes.

They will make each other's beds.

Our children will eat at one long table;
the longest wickedest table we've ever seen.

Our children will bear witness to our history.

Our children will correct our story.

They will put us in their paintings
and display our failures in public hangings.

Our children will reclaim the daytime for the sun.

Our children will shatter glass ceilings with fists made of flowers.

They will stare each other in the eyes when they communicate.

They won't open their mouths.

When we die, our children will live
and it will be so damn hard on them
that someday they too will die.

Hear me now:
uncork your neck and pour out your spirit
my friends, my sisters, my brothers
I say this to you urgently
as a tragic skeleton wrapped in painful comedy.

if it is a sign you are looking for, make your home on highways.

I say this to you my friends, my sisters, my brothers
my sons and daughters.

I do not sleep much these days,
but when I do I dream of you
and of you and of you

and I wake up so confused
because if it wasn't for the Heaven I huddle around me
I worry I'd find myself living in Hell

so thank you to the Heavens for existing right now
thank you, Earth, for gravity
thank you, Wind, for levity
thank you, Water, for movement
and thank you, Fire
for giving us something to circle around.

I say this to you, my friends, my sisters, my brothers

I love you.

I love your death and I love your rebirth.

I love your broken womb, your unwatched fire
your five-course meal of disaster
that you offer me on a dirty platter

and I love you not in the next moment but in this one.

I love your wealth and your company and your energy
for I will die poor and tired and alone.

Every single one of us will die poor and tired and alone.

Thank you to the warm hand that carries my dead skull
home, into this half-haunted apartment
where I close my door and rest

dreaming of everything.

Brice Maiurro is a poet and writer from Denver, Colorado. He is the author of *Stupid Flowers*. He is the Editor-In-Chief of *South Broadway Ghost Society*, and the Poetry Editor of Suspect Press. He has played the hero, the victim and the villain.

bricemaiurro@gmail.com

www.ingramcontent.com/pod-product-compliance
Lightning Source LLC
Chambersburg PA
CBHW020128130526
44591CB00032B/574